The Official Guide
to Living with
DINOS

Jessica Dolce

The Official Guide to Living with DINOS/ Jessica Dolce. —1st ed.
ISBN 978-1-50863-176-7

Contents

Dedicated to all the dogs I've had the pleasure to walk over the years. Especially the naughty ones.

"Stop! My dog is contagious!"

—Everyone who has ever owned a DINOS

Introduction

Around this time three years ago, after a particularly frustrating dog walk, I came home and wrote a blog that would change my life.

That post, titled "My Dog Is Friendly: A Public Service Announcement," was written for the two people who read my Tumblr blog at the time—my mom and my best friend Kelly, who is also a dog walker.

My only goal was to make Kelly, who has the best sense of humor, laugh as I vented some of our shared frustrations with dealing with the dog-owning public.

As dog walkers, we spent nearly every day, all day, walking dogs and encountering all kinds of absurd, rude, and sometimes dangerous behavior. And I'm not talking about the dogs. It was, as all animal care professionals know, the *people* that were the most challenging part of our working day.

On that particular afternoon, I had been chased back and forth across the same city block three times by a woman who insisted that our dogs meet, despite my protests. The dog I was walking was loosely held together by a couple dozen staples after she'd had numerous cancerous growths removed from her belly.

My job for that day was simple: don't let the dog get excited or her staples might pop and she'd turn inside out. Meeting other excited dogs was out of the question. But this other person wouldn't accept a hint, a hand gesture, or me yelling at her to stay away.

This woman wasn't an anomaly. This scenario had been playing out for a decade, like some version of a dog walker's *Groundhog Day*. Tired of it, I went home and wrote.

That post, shared on Facebook just so that my friend could read it, went viral overnight.

By the next morning over 10,000 people had read the post "My Dog Is Friendly." To keep up with demand, I created a new blog to host the post and manage the high traffic. Searching for a name for my new, suddenly popular blog, I titled it the most honest thing I could think of: Notes from a Dog Walker.

Within a week, 50,000 people had read the post. My new readers had enthusiastically grabbed on to a single phrase I had used in the blog:

DINOS™. It's short for Dog(s) in Need of Space.

Having worked with dogs for years, I knew that I had hit a big collective nerve. It wasn't just me and Kelly that were fed up with what we were dealing with on our dog walks. Everyone else was too.

So I started a Facebook page that first week of December 2011, and people from all corners of the world—from Tasmania to Germany to Japan—wrote to tell me that they never knew there was a word for their dogs, but now they knew that they were living with DINOS.

Over the past few years I've continued to write about both the serious and silly aspects of sharing my life with the many DINOS I live and work with every day. Eventually I built a stand-alone website filled with helpful resources.

As time has gone on, the term DINOS has made its way around the globe and is used by dog trainers, animal shelters and businesses, and many other animal care pros. It's left my blog and made its way into *Bark Magazine* and the *Whole Dog Journal,* as well as into all of your homes.

I never imagined any of this.

Thank you to all of you who have come along for this wild ride.

To make things easier for those of you who are brand new to the whole DINOS circus, I thought it was time to finally write this primer on living with DINOS. My hope is that it makes living with DINOS a little less isolating and a whole lot funnier.

To all of you who have been hanging in with me since 2011 (and long before), I'm sending out a love-filled high five to Team DINOS. Thanks for rocking my world.

And a special thanks to Kelly, who never fails to make me laugh, is brilliant at making up new words, and makes me a better, funnier person.

Jessica Dolce
Dog Walker. Writer. Poop Scooper
North Yarmouth, Maine
December 2014

What the Heck Is a DINOS?

If you're reading this, you probably know, but just in case you're not sure if you have a DINOS, let's start at the beginning. Take a look at the blog post I wrote back in 2011 in which I coined the term DINOS. If you've got one, you'll know it after reading this!

My Dog Is Friendly! A Public Service Announcement

There is an epidemic happening across the country and no one is safe. It's occurring on crowded city sidewalks and spacious country walking trails. It doesn't discriminate based on race, age, or economic status.

Innocent dogs and their owners are being terrorized, chased down the street, pinned into corners by...other dog owners.

But, you ask, don't all dogs like to meet, greet, and play with other dogs, even unfamiliar ones? How rude of them not to greet me and my dog! Not so, kind-hearted dog lovers, not so at all.

In every city, town, and suburb, loving, law-abiding families share their lives with dogs that, for a variety of reasons, cannot or would rather not socialize with other dogs.

Today I call on all dog lovers to take a stand on behalf of dogs that walk in public while they simultaneously cope with one or more of the following:

- Contagious diseases
- Leash reactivity
- Service or working dogs
- Injuries and painful physical conditions
- Intolerance of other animals
- Recovery from surgery
- Fearful of unfamiliar or rowdy dogs
- Aging and elderly
- Learning self-control around other dogs
- Are owned by people that want to be left alone

To keep it simple, these dogs and their owners shall be known as Dogs in Need of Space (DINOS).

These DINOS have every right to walk the streets, using a standard 4- to 6-foot leash, without interacting with strangers, human or canine. And yet...they are hounded, day after day, by cheery, well-meaning dog owners who insist on meeting them.

Despite frantic efforts to cross the street or hiding between parked cars, DINOS are chased down by other people walking dogs, who refuse to believe that there is someone out there that does not want to meet them.

How do you spot these terrorists? You can recognize these people by their battle cry, "My dog is friendly!" Henceforth known as My Dog Is Friendly (MDIF).

Pick any corner of any town in America and you're likely to see a scene similar to this one:

A DINOS is working on his manners, let's say it's leash reactivity. He has some issues with strange dogs, but is in training so that he can learn to stay calm in their presence. The DINOS owner spots another dog coming and, like their trainer instructed them, they create some distance and do a sit-stay with eye contact. The goal: to keep cool while the other dog passes.

But they didn't realize they were being stalked by an eager MDIF. Look! There's one now, crossing the street, speed-walking in a beeline right towards the seated DINOS, their own dog straining at the collar.

The DINOS owner steps farther away, trying again to create distance. Any anthropologist (or kindergartner) can read the clear body language in play from the DINOS owner. Observe: no eye contact or smiling, they are facing away from MDIF, perhaps glancing frantically around themselves, looking for an escape.

MDIF is impervious to body language and insists on coming closer. The signals from the DINOS owner become escalated, and like a dog losing its patience with a rude puppy, the DINOS owner issues a quiet but firm warning: "My dog doesn't like other dogs."

Unable to understand their native language, MDIF continues their advances until the DINOS is trapped and begins to lose his ability to stay cool. See: lunging and barking, coupled with awkward struggles to get away. Now, like a dog that's being humped relentlessly by a teenage dog with no manners, the DINOS owner snaps, so the message is clear, "Stop! Don't come any closer!"

And, without fail, MDIF calls out their cheerful, pleading battle cry, "My dog is friendly!" Usually this is received by the back of the DINOS team as they jog away.

Then, with a hurt look, the MDIF mutters, "What's your dog's problem?"

The DINOS owner, shaken, wonders why they are working so hard on improving their dog's manners when the humans around them have the social skills of, well, a dog with no social skills.

A brief interlude from the author:

Quickly, let's turn to the similar epidemic of off-leash dogs that are not under voice control. It's the law: Put your dog on a leash. No one but ME gets to decide who my dog interacts with. Not you, with the "friendly" dog who just wants to say "hi," or you, with the dog who "knows" not to leave your property, but charges me up my porch steps. I, and I alone, will decide if my dog will be interacting with your dog, and when you let your dog run loose you are ROBBING ME of my right to choose whether or not we want to interact with your dog. Not cool.

And now back to our Public Service Announcement:

Dogs In Need Of Space are good dogs. They may not want to socialize with your dog, but they have the right to walk with their owners, on leash, without harassment from strangers who insist on a forced greeting. Their owners do not want to cause a scene or yell, in a panic, at strangers. They don't want their dog to act inappropriately, get hurt, backslide on their training, or frighten anyone. Please, dog lovers of the world, allow these dogs and their people some space and, if they are walking or turning away from you, keep your dog close by and pass them without comment.

All they want is to walk their dogs in peace, without having to hide under a park bench in order to escape the relentless pursuit of dog owners who call out..."My dog is friendly!"

Want a more succinct, less snark-filled explanation?

Here's what a DINOS is:

DINOS are Dogs in Need of Space. The term DINOS is intended to help the public understand that *all* dogs have a need for and a right to their personal space. Some dogs may have a stronger need for space than others.

Dogs might be DINOS for a variety of reasons, such as:
- Medical: illness, injury, surgery, or rehab
- Occupation: Service and Working Dogs
- Training: learning polite leash manners
- Age: issues such as arthritis, vestibular disease, or blindness

- Behavioral: fear, anxiety, reactivity, intolerance of other animals

All DINOS really are different. Some DINOS love other dogs but are recovering from surgery and need space to stay healthy. Some DINOS are afraid of other dogs or strange people and need space to stay calm. Either way, they both need space.

That's the only thing that all DINOS have in common: they need space.

At one time or another, every dog will need space. DINOS is a handy term that serves as a reminder that not all dogs are comfortable or able to interact with unfamiliar dogs or people. That's perfectly normal.

You Know You're Living with DINOS When...

✓ You've whispered "be very, very quiet" to your dog as you tip-toed past a sleeping dog in a yard.

✓ You've jumped a fence, squeezed behind a dumpster, or cut through someone's back yard to avoid an oncoming dog.

✓ You've got your dog trainer on speed dial.

✓ You bought equipment for a home gym, but you already have a gym membership. The treadmill is for the dog.

✓ On your walks, you wear poop bags on your hands, like mittens, so you can scoop and run.

You're Not Alone *or* Welcome to Team DINOS

Here's what I learned that first week after I created DINOS: tens of thousands of you are upset and frustrated by what you encounter on your walks and almost all of you thought you were alone...until you read that blog.

You guys actually thought you were the only one with a dog that needs space. Boy, were you all wrong! For real, if this were a pop quiz, you'd get a big fat F. In red marker.

Within hours of publishing that blog, my Inbox was flooded with hundreds of emails from all around the world from dog owners who were so relieved and grateful to know that they weren't the only ones who were working through similar issues.

And just knowing they weren't all by their lonesome helped so many people feel better. People wrote to tell me that reading the blog and Facebook page provided the support and encouragement they needed to keep on trying each day, despite the challenges.

I heard from people with Service Dogs, fragile senior dogs, deaf dogs, epileptic dogs, blind dogs, and most of all from those of you who live with fearful or reactive dogs. So many of you who live with dogs who have behavioral issues think that you're the only ones who are struggling. Feeling isolated makes everything so much more difficult and overwhelming.

So if nothing else, this book is here to let you all know that you are not and never were alone. In fact, you're a member of a really big tribe.

Welcome to Team DINOS.

We're a club with a lot of members. But we can't stop to say hello to each other, because we're too busy hiding behind a parked car to get some space from you and your dog. We know you understand.

You Know You're Living with DINOS When...

✓ You've mapped out every dog in the neighborhood and refer to houses by the type of dog that lives there (e.g., "off-leash Labs" and "invisible fence Yorkies").

✓ You've yelled "My dog is contagious" to stop people from coming any closer.

✓ Blind corners are scarier than a Hitchcock movie.

✓ You've driven around the block for ten minutes until the field you want to walk in is finally empty.

✓ You've left your dog's poop on the ground because a dog was coming, then circled back to get it when the coast was clear (or picked up another dog's poop as penance).

The Poop Is Always Firmer on the Other Side of the Fence *or* There's No Such Thing as a Perfect Dog

I'm a bad dog owner
My dog is a bad dog
I failed my dog
I wish I had a normal dog
It's not fair that my dog isn't one of the cool kids

Any of those sound familiar? Let's take a look at these common thoughts we use to torture ourselves:

I'm a bad dog owner |My dog is a bad dog | I failed my dog

Secretly, I know that some of you are beating yourself up thinking that you're bad dog owners or that your dogs are bad apples. So let me set the record straight.

You're not a bad person. Your dog isn't a bad dog. Your dog just needs space.

Once you understand that, a lot of things can shift around and you don't have to beat yourself up so much.

Truth is, I hear from so many of you who feel not only isolated, but also ashamed. Even professional dog trainers write me to say that they feel like failures for having their own personal dogs who need space.

Some of you wish you hadn't done stuff in the past because you think it might have contributed to your dog's behavioral issues. In that case, I'll point you to the words of one of the wisest women of all time, the great Maya Angelou, who said, "I did then what I knew how to do. Now that I know better, I do better."

Here's what I think about all of these ways that we torment ourselves:

Let it go. Beating yourself up or feeling badly about yourself or your dog doesn't help. It doesn't make anything better. You know what does?

Understanding, accepting, and attending to your individual dog's needs, recognizing that you and your dog aren't total weirdos (OK, maybe a little), and knowing that a lot of us have walked in your space-needing shoes, so we can help make things easier for you!

I wish I had a normal dog | It's not fair that my dog isn't one of the cool kids

You might be feeling down because your dog isn't matching your expectations of what you thought owning a dog would be like. You really want your dog to be "normal."

Maybe you're stuck thinking about how unfair it is that your dog isn't what you had hoped for or that they're more work than you wanted them to be. Two things:

1. Life is unfair. If life were fair we'd all be rich and have access to clean drinking water. But we don't.

2. There are no perfect dogs out there. All right, maybe there are one or two, but not nearly as many as you think.

The quicker you accept these two things, the faster you can move on to enjoying your life with your dogs.

Here's what I know from my years of working with other people's dogs: Behind closed doors the dogs that look so perfect out on the street (the ones that seemingly don't need space) are peeing in the basement, have a taste for expensive shoes, or are crippled by separation anxiety. They have medical problems and loose poop and weird lumps and are terrible at karaoke.

Ok, not *all* of them, but almost every dog I know has something going on that is really worrying or bothering their owners. I'm not saying this to suggest that all dogs are a hot mess or that dogs are always a pain to own. But you really can't judge a dog by how it looks outside or by its Instagram account.

Don't waste time and energy comparing yourself to other owners and their dogs. In real life or online.

As Teddy Roosevelt so wisely said, "Comparison is the thief of joy."

It's true. Smart guy, huh? He should totally run for president sometime.

Often, the dogs that you're longing to have—the ones that like going to the dog park or love meeting strangers—have their own set of baggage that their owners are dealing with too. And to top that off, even the most well-socialized, happy-go-lucky dogs can wind up becoming DINOS one day.

Truth be told, many DINOS are made, not born. Meaning, when social dogs are subjected to rude, rushed greetings or aggressive incidents at places like doggie day care, dog parks, or just out on the street, then they can lose their tolerance for having other dogs and/or people in their space.

And as dogs get older—forget it! Aching old bones, creaky backs, slow reflexes, and a burning desire to get back home to watch *Antiques Roadshow* will typically lead to old dogs having shorter fuses with young, energetic bucks who get in their bad breath–filled space.

What I'm saying is that anyone might find that their dog became a DINOS overnight after a dog fight or over time as arthritis kicks in. It can happen to anyone, even people with perfect, normal dogs. And it does.

So rather than wasting energy wishing you had a normal dog or a pet unicorn you could ride to work, just take a look at the dog in front of you. Notice the good stuff. Write it down so you'll remember it.

For example, my reactive dog Boogie is housetrained, acts like a gentleman with our three cats, isn't destructive in the house, cuddles like a pro, is low energy, and sleeps late in the morning. These things are awesome and it makes him very easy to live with most of the time.

I know that some dog owners really wish their dogs were like this. So I feel quite lucky to have Boogie, even though he acts like a real fool at the vet's office and on leash sometimes. I try not to spend time wishing he was like any other dog I know, even the ones who love going to the vet.

The poop is always firmer on the other side of the fence, you know?

The sooner we accept that the dog we have is the dog we have, the sooner we can move on to figuring out what they need as individuals to be happy and safe, and the sooner we can connect with them in a more joyful way.

Look for ways to support and celebrate your dogs, so you can enjoy life together...even if that life is a little different than you once imagined it would be.

It's OK to Be Picky About Professional Help

We all need a little help and sometimes that means bringing in the pros. There are so many dog trainers, veterinarians, and dog walkers out there to choose from. Many of them will be just fine for your average dog. But if you have a dog with behavioral challenges, such as fear, reactivity, or aggression, you're probably going to have to shop around until you find the right pros to support you.

That might mean you switch vets or trainers a few times until you connect with the person who is the right fit for you. That's OK! They may be the experts in their fields, but you can still question whether or not they're the right person for your dog and you to be in a relationship with—because that's what it is: a relationship. Date around until you find your happily ever after.

When it comes to veterinarians, I highly recommend reading the online (it's cheaper) version of Dr. Sophia Yin's *Low Stress Handling, Restraint, and Behavior Modification of Dogs and Cats* book. It will help you to better understand what your dogs need to feel safe at the vet so that you can support them. Plus it will help you recognize whether or not your vet's approach is helping or hurting your dogs.

If you'd like some ideas for a vet near you who has a special touch with DINOS, check out the list of veterinarians over on the DINOS website.

As for dog walkers and pet sitters, I wish you could all just hire me and then we'd all be set. But I'm booked and there are thousands of you, so I'll just say this:

You want to know if the dog walker has the skills to work with your dog, and they need to be able to make an informed decision about whether or not they can handle your dog safely. A good dog walker knows their limits. It's OK for them to tell you they aren't skilled enough to work with your behaviorally challenged dog. In fact, it's the responsible thing to do. So don't hide anything from them or sugarcoat stuff.

Before you hire them, ask them over for a meet and greet so you can watch them interact with your dog. Once they're at your house, and you're liking what you see, ask them to take a walk with you and your dog, so you can see them handle your dog outside.

Finally, trainers. Most of us need trainers to help us with our dogs. But finding one can be confusing, and if you've had bad experiences in the past, you may be feeling hesitant to try again. Sara Reusche, professional dog trainer and author of the immensely helpful blog *Paws Abilities*, had this to say when I asked her how to find a good trainer:

> "Talk to the trainer ahead of time and ask them a little bit about their experience and the methods they use. Ask if you can observe a class or a private training session and make sure you're comfortable with that trainer's interactions with dogs and people. The students—both human and canine—should both appear to be having fun and being successful. Look for a trainer who is kind and respects both ends of the leash." [1]

That's good advice. Whether it's a veterinarian or a trainer or a dog walker/pet sitter, they should be respectful of you and your dog. If they do something that makes you feel uncomfortable or their approach isn't working, it's perfectly OK to move on.

Don't worry about hurting their feelings. I mean, you don't have to throw your drink in their face, slap them with your gloves, and yell "Fiend!" But you don't have to keep working with them either. You don't owe them anything.

It's your dogs you need to worry about. And it's up to you to find the right team of pros to support them, so take your time and shop around.

Like the old saying goes: You can pick your team of professionals and you can pick your nose, but you can't pick your pro's nose. Or something smart like that.

To learn more, please see the resource section at the end of the book.

Notes

[1] http://notesfromadogwalker.com/2013/10/21/reactive-dogs-interview-with-sara-reusche/

Gear Up!

One day, when Team DINOS goes to the Olympics, we might have to wear a uniform. I vote for bedazzled Snuggies and platform flip-flops. But until then, there is no requirement for your dogs to wear any flags, colors, or festive hats to be a part of the team.

However, there are some items you might want to get in order to make your life a little easier. Here are some of my favorites:

A Basket Muzzle: Every dog should be comfortable wearing a muzzle. Whether it's because of an emergency or because it'll help everyone stay calm and safe during regular vet exams, muzzles are really helpful tools. Basket muzzles allow dogs to eat, drink, and pant while they wear them, so they can be worn in a variety of situations.

Spray Cheese: This miracle "food" makes a lot of things way less scary. Use it at the vet, in training classes, or when you want to share a snack with your dogs while binging on Netflix. See also: squeeze tubes. Fill small travel tubes with peanut butter, baby food, or other messy, but high-reward treats. This delivery system makes it easy to continuously reward your dogs without pause if you need to distract them in a tight spot.

Spray Shield®: Not sure what to do when an off-leash dog runs up to you? If you're carrying this, you can count on having one tool to deal with it. Get some. Just don't get it mixed up with Spray Cheese or you'll have loose dogs following you around in the hopes of getting sprayed with a face full of cheese.

A Carabiner: There are many ways this can come in handy to help secure your dog. One way to use it is to attach the carabiner to your dog's collar, then hook it to their body or head harness or training collar too. That way if one collar breaks open, you're still connected to each other.

A Hands Free Dog Leash Belt: My favorite belt is from Squishy Face Studios. You simply attach your dog's leash to it and wear the belt around your waist. This frees up your hands to dish out treats, scoop poop, do the robot, and grab chicken bones out of your dog's mouth. It also frees your mind from worrying about dropping the leash if your dog freaks out at another dog. Priceless.

A Fence: If you have a yard, fencing it in will be worth it. There are so many options (in a range of prices) to choose from, plus there are tons of modifications you can make to existing fences to reduce fence fighting, to make them more escape-proof for dogs that are real Houdinis, and to keep other dogs from wandering into your yard.

A T-shirt or Vest for Your Dog that Says: I Need Space: Some people report that these items attract attention (boo! hiss!), but just as many folks say that they help keep people and their dogs away. Yellow ribbons are another option, but so few people know what they are and they can be tough to spot, so they can't always be counted on to help (please note that DINOS is not affiliated with the yellow ribbon campaigns). Personally, I vote for a vest with big words that everyone will understand: Give Me Space.

Poop Bags: When they're full of #2 you can throw them at people who, while reading your dog's *Don't Touch Me!* vest out loud to you, reach out and pet them anyway. It happens.

A Sense of Humor: Never leave home without it.

See the resources section for more on these tips and ideas.

How to Stay Safe on Dog Walks

When you're walking a dog that needs space—either because they're old or they're reactive or they're a service dog—you want to find a place where you won't have to deal with lots of loose dogs or people who let their dogs greet your dog rudely.

Not an easy thing to accomplish, but there are a few basic ways we can stack the deck in our favor:

Walk at odd hours. Most of us are walking very early in the morning and late at night to avoid those peak hours when everyone is out (right before work and in the evenings around dinner time).

As a dog walker, I can say that some busy neighborhoods are pretty empty midday, so it may be worth it to come home at lunch to walk your dogs or hire a dog walker who can come at those times. If you work from home, shift your dog's walks until after your neighbors leave for work.

Walk in odd places. If everyone is at that pretty park or walking the same loop, head in the other direction. Try walking in office building complexes, big box store parking lots, cemeteries, in downtown business districts on weekends, or on busier commercial roads. Not always the most scenic, but often these are more peaceful routes.

Drive to a good spot. Sometimes the safest walking spots aren't right outside our doors. There's nothing wrong with putting your dog in the car and driving them five blocks over to a safer neighborhood or driving fifteen minutes to a quiet park. Never hesitate to drive to a better spot, even if you only need to drive one block to avoid your neighbor's pack of roaming dogs.

Of course, no matter where you go, there's always the possibility of running into a loose dog. Maybe the owner is nowhere to be found, or they're lagging way behind and oblivious to the fact that it's not OK that their dog is chasing you and your dog down. In either case, it's hard not to panic.

The following are some tips for dealing with loose dogs. Keep in mind that nothing works 100% of the time. As the scenarios and dogs vary, so will the solutions.

GENERAL TIPS

Invest in a wardrobe that has generous pockets or a small dog walking bag. On every dog walk bring the following:

- High-value treats
- Cell phone with camera and Animal Control on speed dial
- Spray Shield®
- Optional: One bodyguard (it always helps if you can walk with another person)

Be Quiet. There are a lot of loose dogs hanging out in their yards. The very first thing you can do to avoid a confrontation is to slip by unnoticed. Try crossing to the other side of the street so you're not directly in front of their property. Keep unwanted attention to a minimum by silencing the jingling from your dog's tags with tape or a "pet tag silencer" product.

Engage Your Dog. Sometimes our dogs are the ones attracting the attention when they react to another dog. If you see a dog before (or after) your DINOS does, engage your dog. Keep them focused on you instead of staring or lunging at the other dog. Ask them to "look" at you or check in. Talk to them in a happy, loose voice. Walk briskly. Make kissy sounds. Sing them a silly song with their name in it. Put a treat or toy in front of their nose.

Do whatever you need to do to keep their attention on you as you steer them past the dog hanging out in your neighbor's yard or while you do a U-turn (see below). You can flash a "stop" hand signal at the other dog too, just to reinforce the message that you and your dog aren't interested in them.

For Dogs Behind Fences. If you're passing dogs that are contained and are barking or running the length of the fence, try this: Cross the street to make space and say, "Hi guys!" in a loud and cheery, high-pitched voice. Sometimes that's all it takes to shut them up, and it sends a message to your dog that things are OK.

Lick Your Lips. You need to try to stay calm if you want your dog to stay calm too, so do a body scan. Are you pulling the leash tight? Relax a little. Are you holding your breath? Lick your lips. It's very hard to hold your breath and lick your lips at the same time. Talk in a happy tone. Let your dog know you're cool.

WHEN YOU SEE A LOOSE DOG

In this situation you have two things to deal with—your dog and the oncoming one.

For your dog: Emergency U-Turn. Teach your dog to move quickly and calmly in the opposite direction, so that when you encounter a loose dog or a scary person, you can make a fast getaway. Teach them to do this on cue using a phrase and tone you're most likely to use if you encounter this scenario. Like "Uh-Oh! Let's Go!" or "Holy Sh*t!" Whatever you think you'd actually say.

See Feisty Fido *by Patricia McConnell for more on these techniques, including teaching an emergency sit-stay.*

For the other dog: If you can spot the owner, let them know you need them to leash their dogs NOW in a polite, but firm voice. You may need to fib and tell them your dog is contagious, so they don't just ignore you. Regardless, keep moving via the U-Turn.

IF THE LOOSE DOG IS NOW FOLLOWING YOU

Many of the tips that follow assume that the loose dog is alone and unsupervised. You'll need to use your best judgment, depending on the dog and potential risk involved, but here are a few ideas:

For your dog: Body Block. This means getting in between your dog and the oncoming loose dog. Ideally, you've taught your dog a great sit-stay, so that you can step directly in front of them to deal with the loose dog. Try putting treats right in front of your dog's nose to keep them in place.

For the loose dog, option 1: Use the VOG. That's the Voice of God (a.k.a. what James Earl Jones sounds like). Step in front of your dog and, using the VOG, say NO or STAY and flash the universal hand signal for stop (a flat outstretched palm).

The goal here is to startle the other dog, so you want to really BOOM! If you've got their attention, try telling them to SIT, STAY, or GO HOME.

For the loose dog, option 2: Hurl Treats. Take a handful of those high-value treats you've got in your pocket and throw them right in the other dog's face. The goal here is to startle them, and then have them look around for the food, giving you enough time to get away. You'll likely have a 50/50 success rate with this, so it's worth a try, but it doesn't stop all dogs, particularly those that are aggressive and charging you.

Or toss pea gravel at their feet. If you've got room in your cargo pants for a hand full of pea gravel, it can be worth carrying some to startle oncoming dogs by throwing this at their paws.

IF YOU ARE TRAPPED AND/OR NEED TO ACT VERY QUICKLY

Tools. If your voice and treats don't work and you can't get away (or things are happening so fast you can't think), this is when it's handy to have another tool.

Try carrying one of the following:

- Spray Shield® also known as Direct Stop
- Umbrella (pop-up)
- Air horn
- Shake can (a small tin filled with pennies)
- Walking stick

The idea would be to body block your dog by standing in front of them, and then use any of the tools you have to stop the oncoming dog. Spray 'em, pop the umbrella open in their face, throw the shake can at them, blast the air horn, block them with the stick. Then keep going.

Spray Shield® is a legal citronella spray and it's a great choice. It won't harm the dog, so you're not risking their health. If you use it, spray the dog right in the muzzle. Side note: If the owner *is* nearby and wasn't responding to your request for them to control their dogs, just the sight of the spray may motivate them to take action and get their dogs.

Please practice using the tools. In the chaos of a loose dog interaction, our brains often bail out on us and we forget how to use a tool like the spray. To build confidence and a higher chance of success, you'll want to practice unholstering and spraying. By repeating the movements when you're at ease, you'll build a muscle memory for that action, so that when panic takes over your brain, your body will still remember what to do.

WHEN ALL ELSE FAILS

Here's what some people have done to get their dogs away from loose dogs:

• Thrown their dogs over a fence

• Thrown their dogs over their shoulders, while kneeing or kicking the loose dog

• Thrown their dogs into the bed of random a pick-up truck

The point is, whatever you can think of, it's been done. Do what you have to do to keep everyone safe.

If the two dogs actually do connect, expect a lot of noise. Dogs sound awful when they're in a tussle, but it usually sounds far worse than it actually is. Try to stay calm (so hard, I know), but if you're alone, call for help. A neighbor might come to lend a crucial second set of hands.

If you have a helper, break up the fight by making a loud noise, spraying the dogs with your Spray Shield®, or finding something to use as a physical barrier to smash/slide in between the dogs so that you can safely separate the dogs. Look for something big, like a trash can lid, a chair, a recycling bucket, anything large and nearby that you can wedge between the dogs.

Grabbing collars is an invitation to get bit (your own dog is likely to swing their head around and redirect on you), but sometimes people do it anyway. If you do grab collars, you can try twisting them to cut off air supply—only briefly. Better yet, try holding them by the back legs instead. When you're able to separate the dogs, both parties need to move away from each other, preferably in a wide circle—not straight back—and do not let go of the dogs.

If you are all alone, the truth is that it's really hard to safely break up a dog fight by yourself. When you break up a dog fight you need to make sure that, after the dogs are separated, they don't go right back at each other. One way to do this, if you are by yourself, is to tie one of the dogs to a fence or post (you can also use a carabiner clip to secure the dog to the post, see Lesson 5), separate the dogs, and then do not let go of the one you're holding. Move the dog as far away as you can. If there is any way to tie them up or enclose them (e.g. in an unlocked car or screened in porch), do it. Call for help, call 911.

Things rarely get this far. For the most part, dogs chase you away from their property or chase after you to play or try to start a little bit of trouble, and you can stop them with one of the early tips and tools.

No matter what happens, it's best to think about these things before they occur. Have a plan in place. Know the hot spots in your neighborhood with loose dogs and avoid them, even if you have to take a less convenient route. Walk at off hours. Scope out escape routes. Bring a friend, so you always have a second set of hands. Drive your dogs to a safe spot to walk them.

And if your dog is aggressive, please use a muzzle (see Lesson 5) so you don't have to worry about them hurting a friendly off-leash dog that gets in their face.

RECAP:

- Give all dogs space by moving away from their property.
- Engage your dog. Keep them focused on you and quiet enough not to attract unwanted attention.
- If you see a loose dog, try doing an Emergency U-turn to get away.
- If you're stuck, Body Block your dog, step forward, and use the VOG and/or throw treats at them. Then keep moving away.
- If the dog keeps coming and you feel like there's no escape, spray them with Direct Stop, blow your air horn, use your tools.
- If contact is made, spray the dogs in the muzzle or use whatever large object you have access to (from a stick to trash can lid) to slide in between the dogs.
- Separate the dogs and do not let go. Call for help.
- Go home and have a drink. Don't beat yourself up if the walk went badly. It happens to all of us!

I have to say this: Use these tips at your own risk. The author assumes no responsibility for any harm that may arise from the use of this content. Please contact a professional for further assistance.

You Know You're Living with DINOS When...

✓ You have a preference for the kinds of cars you like to hide behind.

✓ Your hamster's exercise ball is starting to look like a good idea for your dog, if only you could build one large enough for your Lab.

✓ You've set your alarm to go to the dog park at four in the morning.

✓ Your neighbor hasn't looked you in the eye since "that time" that you told her where she could stick her roaming off-leash dog.

How to Exercise at Home plus Meet the Flirt Pole

Despite what you may have heard, you don't always need to leave the house or yard to exercise your dogs. Walking our dogs on leash multiple times a day is a relatively new invention in terms of how we exercise our dogs. There are plenty of other ways to exercise, train, bond with, and work with your dog (and other ways to socialize them out in the world—see Lesson 8).

So if you live in a neighborhood where walking your dog is dangerous (for example, lots of loose dogs) or your dog is so terrified by walks they can't benefit from them, it's time to think outside the walk/box! Focus on exercising and enriching them in other ways each day.

And frankly, there are just some days that you don't want to walk your dog. No matter what kind of dog you have. Maybe it's because the weather is terrible or you have a cold. Some days we could all use a break.

Here are some of my favorite ways to wear out dogs *inside* the house or in your yard:

Treadmills: They can be total lifesavers for DINOS. With a treadmill you can safely exercise your DINOS in your home, with no other dogs to contend with, whenever your dog needs it. You can use the treadmill you already have, purchase a used one for cheap off of Craigslist, or buy a treadmill specifically designed for dogs. You can also use treadmills before a walk to tire your dog out a bit, so that they're more relaxed or more able to focus on training during the walk.

Puppy Push-Ups: Sit, down, sit, down, sit, down. Easiest "trick" in the book. It helps burn off a little energy, even if your dog only knows two commands!

Feeding All Meals in Puzzles: Chuck your dog bowls and try feeding from puzzles or Kongs® instead. There are so many puzzles and interactive toys you can use to turn a 30-second scarf-fest into a 10- to 30-minute activity. If you're using Kongs®, try stuffing them tight with wet kibble or wet food and freezing them. It'll take much longer for your dogs to work out their meal this way. Eating from puzzles burns lots of mental and physical energy (and it keeps them busy so you can read a magazine in peace).

Heavy-Duty Chew Toys and Bones: Some dogs can work out an incredible amount of energy through chewing on toys and bones. Every dog is different and some chews pose a danger to your dog's teeth, but some potential ideas are: Nylabones®, antlers, Himalayan dog chews, raw bones, and bully sticks. This is particularly helpful for barkers, since chewing wears out those overactive jabber jaws.

Teach Em Tricks: You can wear out your dog by working their minds along with their bodies when you teach them tricks. Pick up a good trick book like *101 Dog Tricks* by Kyra Sundance and work on a new trick each week or whenever you're snowed in. Tricks might include stuff like "High Five" or more complicated tricks like "Open the Fridge" or "Change the Oil in the Truck." Not only will your dog get a mental workout, but you'll get to bond with your dog as you work together, and this will make your walks more fun in the future.

Hide and Go Seek: Ask your dog to sit or down and stay or have someone else hold on to them. Leave the room and hide. Call your dog. Wait while they search for you. Give them treats or butt scritches when they find you. Bonus points if your dog is the one who hides.

Fetch: If you have enough space or an empty stairwell, play ball in the house. If you can, have them run up stairs to get their toy and give them a real workout.

Nose Work: Nose work is the best game ever because no dog can fail at it. You can take a class on it if you like, but you can just play at home. Nose Work is all about having fun, no skills necessary. Basically, you throw a few empty cardboard boxes on the floor, put treats in one of them, then bring your dog into the room and tell them to "find it." They will eventually find it because they have...noses. Once they get better at it, you can put a few stinky treats in a yogurt container with a few holes punched in the lid and hide the container around the house for them to find. Please note: you are required to cheer for your dog when they find the treats. See more about Nose Work in Lesson10.

DIY Agility: Got a broom and some books? Then you also have an agility jump. Get creative or just do an internet search for DIY agility sets and turn your house or yard into a sporting arena!

And here's my favorite way to wear out dogs in the yard (you can also try this inside if you have a big room):

The Flirt Pole

Basically, the flirt pole is a giant cat toy. It's an easy DIY project (that you can also buy for around $30, if you hate making stuff) with three parts: PVC pipe, rope, and toy. The flirt pole not only helps your dog work on their basic manners and impulse control, but it also gives them a rockin' workout in just a few minutes. And you hardly have to do a thing. This is a great way to physically and mentally challenge your dogs, without leaving home. This is what you've all been waiting for.

How a Flirt Pole works:

You drag the toy on the ground (and sometimes off the ground a bit) in a big circle. The dog chases the toy and catches it occasionally, then plays tug with it. There are rules to the game.

Why you want to use a Flirt Pole:

1. It totally and completely exhausts dogs in record time. But it doesn't exhaust you.

2. You can use it as a fun way to practice the following commands: sit, down, look, wait, take it, leave it, drop it.

3. You'll be working your dog's rile/recovery skills. That means they'll get to practice listening to you when they're in a state of high arousal (chasing and tugging) and learn to cool off quick (drop it and lie down) when you say so. Handy for reactive dogs who are working on impulse control.

4. You can tire out your dog at home, before going on a walk, so they're more relaxed.

5. You can tire out your dog at home, instead of going on a walk, so you're more relaxed.

6. You can make a small flirt pole (half the regular size) and use it inside the house, if you don't have a yard.

How to make a Flirt Pole:

1. For a medium to large dog, buy a 4- to 6-foot-long 3/4" PVC pipe, 10–15 feet of rope, and a soft dog toy.

2. Thread the rope through the pipe and tie a knot at either end of the pipe, to keep rope from sliding in and out.

3. Tie the toy to the end of the rope.

4. Optional: buy fun colored electrical tape (finally an excuse to buy lime-green tape!) and wrap the PVC pipe so it's all fancy schmancy pants.

Flirt Pole rules you will use:

1. Dog must lie down, look at you, leave the toy alone, and wait for you to release them, before playing.

2. When you tell them to "take it," then they get to chase the toy as you drag it around.

3. After a few pass-bys, reward them by allowing them to catch the toy.

4. Let them tug until you tell them to "drop it."

5. Have them lie back down and wait until they are totally calm. Then start again.

6. Change direction every once in a while, so your dog isn't always running one way.

7. If the dog grabs the toy before you say "take it" or is mouthy or jumping on you: take a time out and/or start over.

When to skip the Flirt Pole:

1. If your dog has bad joints or injuries that could be aggravated by quick changes of direction and jumping.

2. If your dog doesn't know the following: wait, take it, leave it, drop it. Practice with treats first, then a tug toy, then move on to the flirt pole.

3. If you do not know the dog well. It's not safe to rev up an unfamiliar dog. While this is one of my all-time favorite tools for shelter dogs (it tires them out so fast!), they must know basic commands and you need to have a relationship with the dog, before getting them super psyched. Establish a working bond first—make sure you're communicating with each other— then start off slow.

4. If this overstimulates your dog to the point that they can't calm down after. You know your dogs. If this isn't a good fit for them, just pass.

5. If your dog thinks it's dumb. Some dogs just don't dig it.

6. Still not sure what to do? See the resources section for more info.

No matter what your reasons are, adding some fun and challenging activities like these into your routine will make your walks (or lack thereof) much more pleasant for you and your dogs, so get creative at home!

Socialization Doesn't Have to Be a Direct Contact Sport *or* Dog Parks Aren't the Only Game in Town

So now you might be asking, if I'm avoiding dogs on my walks or exercising my dog at home, how do I socialize them? There's a misconception among most dog owners these days that the right way or the *only* way to socialize dogs is by letting them play off leash together. Not so, Team DINOS (or anyone else)!

Socializing happens whenever dogs are spending time together, even when they're on leash.

Think about it human terms—if the only way we could be social was to go to a rave, we'd be a bunch of poorly socialized nuts wearing giant pants and glitter. Luckily, we don't need to go to an all-night dance party to be social. Every time we leave the house and stand in a line at a store or go to work in our offices or enjoy a meal at a restaurant, we're being social with other humans.

It doesn't have to be direct contact in order to be socializing.

Same with our dogs. Many dogs not only do better in more structured and supervised social outings than the rodeo that is the dog park, they actually *prefer* it.

So if you want to help your dog to remain social for life or you want to build up some new social skills remember this: Start small, go slow, and keep it supervised.

Here are four ideas to help you safely socialize your dogs:

Take a group training class. When dogs are working and learning side by side (even if they're spread far apart), they're socializing in a structured environment.

Join a dog walking social group. Structured, on-leash group walks can be an awesome way to socialize your dog and keep practicing the skills you've learned in a training class. Plus you get to meet nice folks and take hikes. Check out the DINOS website to see if there's a group near you.

Invite a friend or three to join you and your dog for play dates. Invite them over to your backyard or a safe area for an off-leash play session. Or just go for a walk. Not sure who to ask? Start by taking a group training class or a walk with a social group and check out your fellow participants. Then ask them out! Small-group, supervised off-leash play is fun and much safer than going to the mosh pit, er, dog park.

Foster dogs for a reputable shelter or rescue. If you're comfortable doing it, consider bringing dogs into your home and fostering them until they're adopted. In doing so, you'll be bringing in a steady stream of compatible dogs for your dog to meet and play with (just remember: go slow, do not rush introductions, and know your dog—not all dogs like having other dogs in the house, but some will really love it!). Partner with a reputable shelter or rescue that will help you find the right matches for your dog.

Speaking of being social, let's talk about how you can make human friends when your dog needs space. It's pretty easy to meet other dog owners at the dog park, but what do you do when you can't hang out at the Thunderdome?

I'd suggest any of the ideas on the previous page (there will be people involved in all those situations) and one more: volunteer.

Volunteer at the animal shelter or at a soup kitchen or at a farm stand. Find what you love, pick a nonprofit that does that, start volunteering, and you'll meet other people who are big hearted, just like you!

You Know You're Living with DINOS When...

✓ You've considered adding "excellent horizon scanner" to the skills section of your resume.

✓ You've stood around, pretending to admire someone's mailbox, while trying to keep enough distance between you and the slow-moving dog ahead.

✓ If you win the lottery, you're buying a private dog park.

✓ Your heart skips a beat when a front door or garage door opens just as you walk past a house.

Stop Caring What Everyone Else Thinks and Stand Up For Your Dog

The following is one of my most popular blog posts of all time. If you ignore everything else in this book, please make this the one thing you take to heart. It's super important and it's the key to reducing stress and dog bites, keeping everyone around you safe, and being responsible for your dogs.

You need to stop caring what everyone else thinks about you and your dog.

If you do this, you will free yourself up to make better choices on behalf of your dogs. When you make better choices, you are setting your dogs up for success in our crazy world. And when you do that, they are less likely to get into trouble which they will wind up paying for big time.

Here's what you need to do:

1. Stand up for your dogs. Be assertive in protecting your dog's physical and mental health, as well as the safety of those around them.

2. When you're not sure if your dog can handle something, always err on the side of caution. Choose management over "I don't know, so let's find out!"

Dogs need us to do both of these things more often, so that they don't feel like they need to take matters into their own hands, er, teeth.

Obviously, dogs need lots of other things from us too: socialization, training, proper management, and a never-ending supply of peanut butter that they can roll around in like it's a canine version of that scene in *Indecent Proposal.* People also need to learn how to read their dog's body language, understand stress and fear, and not screw their dogs up in general. But all of that has been covered by lots of other dog professionals.

What I'm talking about now doesn't really have all that much to do with the dogs. It's about us *humans* and how uncomfortable many of us are with being forceful, direct, and making unpopular choices that we're afraid will make people not like us. This is causing some problems for our dogs.

Too often we choose not to speak up for our dogs, even as things take a weird turn. We recognize that our dog is uncomfortable with the hyper kids running circles around them. We suspect that the unfamiliar dog approaching our dog isn't as friendly as their owner is claiming. We don't know if our dog is OK with the cleaning lady entering the house while we're gone. But we allow it anyway.

We allow our desire to be perceived as friendly or nice or easy-going to override our own gut instincts or what our dog is trying to tell us. Our desire to be liked—to avoid being seen as unfriendly or rude or "bitchy"—is powerful stuff.

It's so powerful that humans will choose to ignore their own instincts and proceed into potentially dangerous scenarios, just so they don't make a bad impression.

Gavin de Becker, author of *The Gift of Fear*, says that unlike other living creatures, humans will sense danger, yet still walk right into it. "You're in a hallway waiting for an elevator late at night. Elevator door opens, and there's a guy inside, and he makes you afraid. You don't know why, you don't know what it is. Some memory of this building—whatever it may be. And many women will stand there and look at that guy and say, 'Oh, I don't want to think like that. I don't want to be the kind of person who lets the door close in his face. I've got to be nice. I don't want him to think I'm not nice'." [1]

If we're willing to walk right into a metal box with a stranger that totally scares us just so we won't be seen as rude, imagine how difficult it is for many people to be assertive on behalf of their dogs with nice folks at the park, neighbors, visitors, family, and friends. We're willing to deny our fear around murderers. It's no wonder we're not comfortable speaking up for ourselves around people we pass on a dog walk.

The problem with our discomfort is that dog bites often happen when:

1. We are in denial about our dog's limitations and/or their behavior issues. For us to be a good advocate for them, dogs need you to see them as they are, in the present.

2. We know their limits, but we still hesitate to take action.

And the flip side of suspecting or knowing your dog has issues and not speaking up is:

3. When we are in complete denial that our "good" dogs would ever bite someone.

Number 3 is a whole book in and of itself. This lesson is really about the first two points. But I'll sum up #3 real quick for good measure:

All dogs have the potential to bite. ALL of them. Breed, size, age, zodiac sign—doesn't matter. Push any dog hard and long enough or in just the right way (You mean it's not OK for my 2-year-old to crawl into my "good" dog's crate while he's sleeping?) and they'll run out of options and will bite. So don't push any dog's luck. Don't allow them to be treated roughly or inappropriately or fail to properly supervise them because they're such "good dogs." Your dog needs you to stop thinking they're a robot with no limits and respect their boundaries. Don't fool yourself.

Your dog will appreciate it if you help them out by setting them up to be good.

When we let dogs bite, the dogs pay for it. They might hurt a person or another dog or get hurt themselves. They might cause your home-owner's insurance to drop you and then you can't keep your dog. They might be declared dangerous. They might make the news and inflame the public into calling for a ban on all dogs that look like your dog. They might be taken from you and euthanized.

Dog bites aren't the only consequence, of course. When we don't step up, other not-so-great stuff happens, like we put our dogs into situations that make them stressed and miserable. Or they have a bad experience with another dog and then they become a DINOS. But this post isn't about dog behavior. It's about us and our malfunctions.

Sometimes, we have to step out of our comfort zone in order to be effective advocates for our dog's safety and health. Do not let others pressure you. Stop caring what anyone else thinks and just do what you know is right for your dogs.

Now, I recognize that there are things that happen that are beyond our control. Also, I understand that sometimes we genuinely think we're making the right choice and it turns out to be the wrong one. And of course, I want you to socialize, train, and do new stuff with your dogs, which means that inevitably there will be goof-ups. I get it. That's life.

What I'm talking about here is when you're hesitant to do what you know needs to be done or when you're afraid to err on the side of caution because you think it'll make you like a "square."

So here's what I'm going to do. I'm going to give you all permission to stand up for yourselves and your dogs. You have to do it. Your dogs need you to do it.

The next time someone tries to force themselves or their dog onto your dog, you're going to boldly step in front of your dogs and say "STOP." Say it like you mean it. Then drop the mic and walk away.

The next time someone comes over to your house and you're not sure if your dog will be OK with them, you're going to put your dog in another room or in their crate or on a leash. When your friend visits with their

little kids or the landscaper needs to use your bathroom or the police*
bangs on your door, you're not going to hold your breath and see what
happens. You're going to tighten up your core muscles and say, "Please
wait while I put my dog away." When they say, "It's OK, I love dogs," you
will hold your ground and follow through with the plan.

And the next time you're at the vet or the groomers and you don't like
the way they're handling your dog, you're going to say, "We need to do
this another way." I struggled with this one. But I'm over it now. Same
thing goes for trainers. If you don't like the way a trainer is working with
your dog, you're going to say, "Thanks, but we need something different."

Yes, the other person may say nasty things to you or about you. They
might call you a "bitch." I want you to not care. Because in that moment
what you really are is your dog's hero. You just took their well-being into
your hands and acted with conviction. You made the right choice and
they're safe because of you. Bravo.

And who cares what people call you? As my future BFF Tina Fey says,
"Bitches get stuff done. Bitch is the new black."

Look, the other person will get over it. They might not even care at
all. For them, the discomfort of dealing with hero-you won't last long.
Even if it does, even if your neighbors think you're kind of stand-off-ish,
it's not rocking their world. But for you, the consequences of not standing
up for your dogs might be long-lasting and deep-cutting. Set those limits,
then don't give a hoot what anyone thinks about you.

P.S. There are other ways to set limits and not giving a crap what anyone thinks, like: if they need it, walk your dog with a muzzle on. You
will get weird looks. But you don't care, cuz you're being Safety First.

Hey, I know this is uncomfortable for some of you. But I know you
can do it because you love your dogs.

If it helps, I want you to think of me standing next to you, cheering
you on as you stand up for your dog's needs. I'm five feet worth of New
Jersey/Philly-loud-talking-feistiness and I don't give an eff about saying
"No" to anyone if it means making sure my dogs don't get into trouble or
have a bad experience. So picture me there beside you the next time you

need a boost. Know that every time you make that tough choice to stand up for your dogs, I'm yelling, "Rock Star!!" just for you.

Now go get 'em, Tiger.

You have the right to secure your dog before letting the police enter your property. ALWAYS do it.

Notes

1   http://www.oprah.com/relationships/Trusting-Your-Intuition-Could-Save-Your-Life

Don't Forget to Have Fun and Treat Yo' Self!

Life with DINOS can be isolating, frustrating, and to be totally honest, some days it's a real bummer. I know how stressed out, overwhelmed, and alone you guys feel sometimes.

And as a bonus, those of us with fearful or reactive dogs are intimately familiar with feeling like failures. We're doing everything we can to help our dogs and make good choices, but things still go sideways sometimes. We show up for a training class or go for a walk and our dogs have a meltdown. Or we have a meltdown. And then we go home stressed and sad.

Depending on what kind of issues you and your dogs are working on—medical, behavioral, or otherwise—there may not be a quick fix or any fix at all. Helping dogs learn how to stay calm on walks or rehabbing a physical injury take time. Often, our dogs need extra help and space for many months or even years. For some dogs, such as those with a medical issue like epilepsy, they'll need space for life.

So what does that mean for you? You gotta relax and have some fun. Like right now.

So put this book down, turn up the Hall and Oates, and start jamming out. Go ahead, I'll wait. OK, put on Beyoncé then. Just dance! Bonus points if your dog dances with you.

You can't wait until your dog is "all better" to start enjoying them or having some good times on your own.

If your whole relationship with your dog is focused on what's wrong with them or what needs improving or all the sacrificing you do for them, there won't be a whole lot of joy.

And trust me, your dog wants you to be happy. Happy people keep their dogs.

You have to find ways to have fun—either together or separately—so that you don't wind up resenting your dog or burning out as a caregiver. Those good times will be what restores you, so that you can go back to working with them and face more insane dog walks.

I hereby command you to look for ways to add some stress-free time back into your life.

#1 Find something fun to do *with* your dog.

I vote for Nose Work. It's a sport that no dog can fail at. It doesn't matter if they're blind, reactive, and only have one leg. They don't need to be well trained or listen to you or even like you. Any dog can succeed at Nose Work games.

All they have to do is sniff around until they find the hidden treats or scents. You can do this at home or take a class. It can be very easy, or if you and your dog are loving this sport, it can increase in difficulty. Dogs can graduate from searching for treats to scents hidden outside. There are even cool titles you can earn!

Classes are often set up so that only one dog is in the room at a time, so if your dog isn't OK around other dogs, that's not a big deal. If you want to learn more about Nose Works check out the resources at the end of the book.

The reason why I love it so much is that you'll have fun, your dog will succeed, you'll bond with one another, and if you take a class, you'll connect with other people who get to see your DINOS at their best. That feels so good. I know tons of Team DINOS members who count Nose Work as their favorite thing to do with their dogs and one of the most helpful.

Bonus tip: After dogs learn "find it!" in class, you can try tossing treats on the ground during walks to give them something to do that will distract them from noticing other dogs nearby or random bothersome stuff.

#2 Don't feel bad about taking some time away from your dogs so you can have fun *without them*.

If you have one very easy-going dog who is a pleasure to walk, but your other dog is a DINOS who makes walks stressful, leave your DINOS at home every once in a while and just enjoy a relaxed walk with your other dog. You both deserve it and your DINOS will get over it. They'll probably enjoy some time home alone so they can finally watch *Mob Wives* in peace.

If you haven't taken a vacation in eons, start researching great pet sitters or boarding facilities or look for a vacation rental that allows dogs and go away!

While I've found that vacationing with my DINOS in the woods of Maine each summer is really fun, I also leave them at home when I travel sometimes. These trips away from being a caregiver to my pets are good for me! I need a break sometimes and so do you.

It doesn't just have to be vacations. If you want to go to a local event —like a festival or farmers' market or even a pet-centric event—and you know your dog will be stressed out there, just leave them at home and go! Enjoy an afternoon away from them. They'll live.

Take care of yourself, so that you'll be refreshed and happy when you come home to take care of your dogs.

You know what the flight attendants say on airplanes, right? Put your own oxygen mask on first. That's what taking little breaks or vacations or putting your dog in a crate for 30 minutes with a puzzle toy while you do yoga without them scooting across your mat means.

And please, above all else, be kind to yourself. There will always be bumps in the road when it comes to living with DINOS, but you'll just keep doing the best that you can. Having compassion and caring for yourself is the foundation of being a patient, loving, and committed member of Team DINOS. Be well and have some fun!

You Know You're Living with DINOS When...

✓ Your dog walking equipment consists of a leash, poop bags, high-value treats, a cell phone, and...a head lamp, so you can walk your dog before the sun comes up.

✓ When you hit the brakes, empty cans of Spray Shield® roll out from under your car seats.

✓ You drive your entire dog walking route to search for any trouble spots before going for a walk.

✓ The unexpected sound of the mailman's keys jingling makes your stomach do a back flip.

Our Message, Our Demands

We want a lot of things: private dog parks, invisible force fields to stop loose dogs from reaching us, people who obey leash laws, a robot that scoops poop and defends us from rogue would-be space invaders, a never ending supply of cupcakes, and the metabolism of a hummingbird. Like I said, lots of stuff.

But when we boil it all down, what we really want is for other people to be responsible and respectful.

We're not asking anyone to be responsible for our dogs. That's our job. We're in charge of keeping our dogs safe, as well as ensuring the safety of those around us. But we are asking that others take responsibility for their actions as well.

The message of DINOS is really meant to encourage all dog owners to be responsible and respectful towards others. This includes having control over our dogs and obeying leash laws.

So as you go forward in your new life as a member of Team DINOS, here's a polite demand that we can all repeat until the rest of the world finally hears our battle cry:

Ask First!

Why *Ask First?* Because someone needs to teach the public not to assume that it's OK for them or their dogs or kids to approach a dog without asking first.

It's never all right to assume it's OK to approach an unfamiliar dog without asking permission first. And dog owners have a right to say "no" if they feel an interaction is not in the best interests of their dogs. We must be respectful of that right to decline.

When we assume that another dog will be OK if we allow our loose dog to chase after them or we let our leashed dog pull us over to say "hi", we're making a judgment call without all the facts. And in doing so we are taking away that other person's right to choose what's best for their dogs.

By training people to pause and ask just one question, "Can I/my dog/my kid say hello to your dog?" we're helping them to be respectful of others, responsible for their actions, and put safety first.

By the way, dogs don't have to be a DINOS for this to idea to apply. Even dogs that are really social and able to meet others at almost any time deserve to be treated with respect. And all dog owners have a right to say, "No, thank you," for whatever reasons they choose.

It's our right as dog owners to decide what's best for our individual dogs and ourselves. Asking first allows all of us to make that choice.

Frankly, it's impossible to know what's going on in another person's world just by looking at them and their dogs. That's why we need to remind dog owners to take responsibility for their actions all the time, around *all* dogs.

If they're reminded often, perhaps more folks will remember to pause long enough to ask permission before they let their dogs (or themselves) run over to say "hi" to a dog. They'll stop making assumptions and start making responsible choices. Let's help them build that habit. And when someone remembers to ask you first, be sure to thank them.

This new habit doesn't just apply to how we want people to behave around our own dogs. All of us who own dogs need to consider how our actions impact everyone around us in the community, including children, the elderly, the disabled, and those with phobias of dogs. We all have a right to safely enjoy public spaces.

Ask First! is a reminder to be respectful of others. Pause and ask first before you let your dog greet another dog walking by on leash. Pause and ask first before you let your dog run up to a senior citizen in a park or a fellow hiker on a trail. Pause and ask first before you reach down to pet a dog in the vet's waiting room.

Just ask first. It's respectful, responsible, safe, and it's the compassionate thing to do. We're all in this boat together and our actions have a huge impact on one another. Let's do our best to be considerate of the needs of others. After all, as Ram Dass said, "We're all just walking each other home."

You Know You're Living with DINOS When...

✓ You've crossed the same block more than three times to avoid other dogs.

✓ You're excited to walk dogs in the rain or snow, since bad weather means fewer dogs to bump into.

✓ You're considering teaching your Great Dane how to use the toilet.

✓ You think Plastic Man and Inspector Gadget were onto something with those extra-long arms. Perfect for catching off-leash dogs at a distance!

The DINOS Website

If you'd like to learn more about some of the tools and tips I've shared here, please visit the DINOS website. I've created a special page that accompanies the lessons in this book. You'll find links to more information on flirt poles, carabiners, breaking up dog fisticuffs, Nose Works, choosing professional help, fences, and great stories from other DINOS families, plus so much more on this page that I've created just for you.

You can access those resources here:

http://dogsinneedofspace.com/book-resources

I also have a couple of blogs and websites you can click through at your reading pleasure.

For more on general dog stuff and lots of poop jokes, plus the occasional look into my animal-filled work and home life, you can find me over at: NotesfromaDogWalker.com

For more DINOS resources, including regularly updated lists of veterinarians, group training classes, boarding facilities, dog walking groups, supplements, videos, and training books that Team DINOS members use and love please see:

DogsinNeedofSpace.com

In addition to all of those nifty resources, you'll also find free handouts and the super cool *Ask First!* Poster there too, so there's no excuse not to visit. Go. Right now.

To get a laugh and meet the rest of Team DINOS, come say hi over on the DINOS: Dogs In Need of Space Facebook page. We'd love to meet you!

MEET THE COVER MODEL

Who's that gorgeous dog on the cover? She's a real life DINOS named Willow. Willow is a good dog who sometimes needs space from people. While she's quick to befriend other animals, Willow prefers to get to know new humans slowly. When she's ready, Willow will invite you into her world. It's a very special place to be.

My deepest thanks to her folks, Nat and Bill, for allowing their brave girl to be a part of the DINOS book. You can follow Willow's adventures with her family and friends at: 365doghikes.com

ABOUT THE AUTHOR

Jessica Dolce is the creator of DINOS™: Dogs in Need of Space and the author of the blog *Notes From a Dog Walker.* A professional dog walker, writer, and teacher, Jessica lives in Maine with her husband, three cats, and two DINOS. You can find more of her work at: JessicaDolce.com